ONE BODY, ONE SPIRIT

BUILDING RELATIONSHIPS IN THE CHURCH

12 Studies for Individuals or Groups

DALE & SANDY LARSEN

Harold Shaw Publishers • Wheaton, Illinois

ISBN-13: 978-0-877-88619-8

Cover photo © 1994 by Robert McKendrick

99 98
                    146502721

CONTENTS

Introduction   5

How to Use This Studyguide   7

1   That All of Them May Be One   11
John 17

2   The Do-ers and the Don't-ers   16
Romans 14:1-4

3   Can We Judge Another's Motives?   21
Romans 14:5-12

4   What If We See a Christian Sinning?   26
1 Corinthians 5; 2 Corinthians 2:5-11

5   Can't I Do What I Want to Do?   31
Romans 14:13-18

6   What Does Stumbling Mean?   35
Romans 14:19-23

7   Following Jesus' Example   40
Romans 15:1-7

8   But Don't I Know Best?   44
1 Corinthians 8:1-8

9   When Do I Give In?   49
1 Corinthians 8:9-13

10   Why Do Eyes Need Ears?   54
1 Corinthians 12:12-26

11   What Happens If I Don't Forgive?   59
Ephesians 4:25-32

12   Is Tension Healthy?   63
Galatians 5:13-26

Leader's Notes   67

INTRODUCTION

" . . . that all of them may be one."

When the eleven disciples in the upper room heard Jesus pray these words, they might have been shamefaced. Hadn't they recently been arguing about which of them was the most prominent?

They could hardly have imagined the millions who would follow Christ in coming centuries throughout continents they'd never heard of! Was Jesus praying that all *these* would be "one"? Could such a prayer be more than wishful thinking?

Christ did pray for complete unity among his followers. He asked God "that they may be one as we are one. . . . May they be brought to complete unity" (John 17:22-23).

Unity among Christians? Does that mean we all have to:

- merge into one superchurch?
- celebrate Communion exactly the same way?
- say identical prayers?
- sing the same kind of music?
- meet in the same building?
- never differ on points of theology?

No! The Holy Spirit recognizes and allows for individual differences of conscience and practice among believers, as your group will find in this study.

What Jesus prayed for and taught, and what Paul wrote about with fervor and vivid imagery, is not so much *conformity* among believers as *oneness*. It's a unity of *attitude* and *heart* rather than a unity of practice.

Oneness of practice could be accomplished mechanically if all of us accepted (or were forced into) the same "rule book" of how we should worship God and carry out our Christian lives.

Oneness of attitude is a spiritual matter. It is first of all inward. No external organization or church structure can produce a heart attitude of love for one another. The Holy Spirit must produce it as we recognize that in Christ we are already one body.

Whether members of your study group tend to think alike or come from widely diverse backgrounds, you'll be blessed as you discover your unity in Christ—a unity that transcends individual differences. "May the God who gives endurance and encouragement give you a spirit of unity among yourselves as you follow Christ Jesus, so that with one heart and mouth you may glorify the God and Father of our Lord Jesus Christ" (Romans 15:5-6).

HOW TO USE THIS STUDYGUIDE

Fisherman studyguides are based on the inductive approach to Bible study. Inductive study is discovery study; we discover what the Bible says as we ask questions about its content and search for answers. This is quite different from the process in which a teacher *tells* a group *about* the Bible and what it means and what to do about it. In inductive study God speaks directly to each of us through his Word.

A group functions best when a leader keeps the discussion on target, but this leader is neither the teacher nor the "answer person." A leader's responsibility is to *ask*—not *tell*. The answers come from the text itself as group members examine, discuss, and think together about the passage.

There are four kinds of questions in each study. The first is an *approach question*. Used before the Bible passage is read, this question breaks the ice and helps you focus on the topic of the Bible study. It begins to reveal where thoughts and feelings need to be transformed by Scripture.

Some of the earlier questions in each study are *observation questions* designed to help you find out basic facts—who, what, where, when, and how.

When you know what the Bible says you need to ask, *What does it mean?* These *interpretation questions* help you to discover the writer's basic message.

Application questions ask, *What does it mean to me?* They challenge you to live out the Scripture's life-transforming message.

Fisherman studyguides provide spaces between questions for jotting down responses and related questions you would like to raise in the group. Each group member should have a copy of the studyguide and may take a turn in leading the group.

For consistency, Fisherman guides are written from the *New International Version*. But a group should feel free to use the NIV or any other accurate, modern translation of the Bible such as the *New Living Translation*, the *New Revised Standard Version*, the *New Jerusalem Bible*, or the *Good News Bible*. (Other paraphrases of the Bible may be referred to when additional help is needed.) Bible commentaries should not be brought to a Bible study because they tend to dampen discussion and keep people from thinking for themselves.

SUGGESTIONS FOR GROUP LEADERS

1. Read and study the Bible passage thoroughly beforehand, grasping its themes and applying its teachings for yourself. Pray that the Holy Spirit will "guide you into truth" so that your leadership will guide others.

2. If the studyguide's questions ever seem ambiguous or unnatural to you, rephrase them, feeling free to add others that seem necessary to bring out the meaning of a verse.

3. Begin (and end) the study promptly. Start by asking someone to pray for God's help. Remember, the Holy Spirit is the teacher, not you!

4. Ask for volunteers to read the passages out loud.

5. As you ask the studyguide's questions in sequence, encourage everyone to participate in the discussion. If some are silent, ask, "What do you think, Heather?" or, "Dan, what can you add to that answer?" or suggest, "Let's have an answer from someone who hasn't spoken up yet."

6. If a question comes up that you can't answer, don't be afraid to admit that you're baffled! Assign the topic as a research project for someone to report on next week.

7. Keep the discussion moving and focused. Though tangents will inevitably be introduced, you can bring the discussion back to the topic at hand. Learn to pace the discussion so that you finish a study each session you meet.

8. Don't be afraid of silences: some questions take time to answer and some people need time to gather courage to speak. If silence persists, rephrase your question, but resist the temptation to answer it yourself.

9. If someone comes up with an answer that is clearly illogical or unbiblical, ask him or her for further clarification: "What verse suggests that to you?"

10. Discourage Bible-hopping and overuse of cross-references. Learn all you can from *this* passage, along with a few important references suggested in the studyguide.

11. Some questions are marked with a ◆. This indicates that further information is available in the Leader's Notes at the back of the guide.

12. For further information on getting a new Bible study group started and keeping it functioning effectively, read Gladys Hunt's *You Can Start a Bible Study Group* and *Pilgrims in Progress: Growing through Groups* by Jim and Carol Plueddemann.

SUGGESTIONS FOR GROUP MEMBERS

1. Learn and apply the following ground rules for effective Bible study. (If new members join the group later, review these guidelines with the whole group.)

2. Remember that your goal is to learn all that you can *from the Bible passage being studied.* Let it speak for itself without using Bible commentaries or other Bible passages. There is more than enough in each assigned passage to keep your group productively occupied for one session. Sticking to the passage saves the group from insecurity and confusion.

3. Avoid the temptation to bring up those fascinating tangents that don't really grow out of the passage you are discussing. If the topic is of common interest, you can bring it up later in informal conversation following the study. Meanwhile, help each other stick to the subject!

4. Encourage each other to participate. People remember best what they discover and verbalize for themselves. Some people are naturally shyer than others, or they may be afraid of making a mistake. If your discussion is free and friendly and you show real interest in what other group members think and feel, they will be more likely to speak up. Remember, the more people involved in a discussion, the richer it will be.

5. Guard yourself from answering too many questions or talking too much. Give others a chance to express themselves. If you are one who participates easily, discipline yourself by counting to ten before you open your mouth!

6. Make personal, honest applications and commit yourself to letting God's Word change you.

THAT ALL OF THEM MAY BE ONE

John 17

How dull life would be without diversity. Distinctive differences offer us a richness of viewpoints and broader perspectives. In the body of Christ diversity is also to be celebrated. But if there is no foundational factor, differences all too often lapse into disharmony and discord.

Just before his death, Jesus prayed specifically that his followers would be "one." He prayed for the faltering and bewildered disciples who were still with him, as well as for all his future followers. That means Jesus prayed for us—for you, your group, all the Christians in all the churches in your town, and the church universal. This oneness Jesus desired for us allows for diversity, but calls for unity in the essentials of the faith.

   1. Give examples of Christian unity and disunity that you have experienced.

Read John 17.

2. Mention several words or phrases that describe the feeling or tone of Jesus' prayer.

3. What do we learn about Jesus' authority and origin from verses 1-5?

♦ **4.** On what basis can any person claim to belong to God and have eternal life?

5. For whom did Jesus pray (verses 9, 20)?

◆ **6.** For whom did Jesus *not* pray? Does this mean he had no concern for the world? Explain.

7. Note what Jesus had "given" to his disciples. What pattern do you see in how and what Jesus gives?

8. According to verses 9-12, what did Jesus specifically pray for in connection with our oneness, and why might we especially need this?

9. What important outcome did Jesus pray for as a result of his followers' unity (verses 20-26)?

10. Why might evidence of unity among Christians produce this outcome?

11. List some of the various churches and Christian organizations in your community (or just in your Bible study). What do all those groups have in common?

12. There have been, and continue to be, innumerable styles and traditions of belief and worship centered on Jesus Christ. How can Jesus' prayer for unity be answered in the midst of such diversity?

13. What can you do, either individually or as a study group, to recognize and strengthen your oneness in Christ?

THE DO-ERS AND THE DON'T-ERS

Romans 14:1-4

In one of the apostle Paul's prayers for unity among believers, he includes a request for endurance and encouragement as they follow Christ.

"Endurance!" you say. "That's what I need all right—to endure those nagging legalistic Christians who try to lay guilt on me for enjoying life! I'm a DO-er. I like to emphasize the positive!"

Or "Encouragement!" you think. "Do I ever need it—encouragement to stick with my beliefs even when other Christians laugh at my scruples and say I take my faith too seriously! I'm a DON'T-er. It's important to be *different* as a Christian!"

The DO-ers and the DON'T-ers . . . will they ever get together? In one sense you can't keep them apart. They always wind up in the same churches, on the same committees, in the same Bible study groups. But will they ever stop contending for their favorite issues and condemning each other?

1. Check off one or more phrases to complete this statement:

I feel uncomfortable around Christians who . . .

___ don't let their kids celebrate Halloween.
___ protest at abortion clinics.
___ recite prayers from a book in their worship services.
___ say women have to wear dresses all the time.
___ speak in tongues.
___ are social drinkers.
___ are too liberal.
___ are too conservative.
___ won't support a Christian school.
___ other:

Briefly explain why this makes you uncomfortable, and on what you base your objections.

Read Romans 14:1-4.

♦ **2.** Paul assumes there will be disputable matters in the church. What general issue were these Christians apparently debating over?

3. What wrong attitude might an "eat-everything" Christian have toward a vegetarian? What wrong attitude might a vegetarian have toward an "eat-everything" person?

4. Are you tempted toward either of those wrong attitudes? Give examples.

♦ **5.** What is meant by one "whose faith is weak"? What is *not* meant by this description?

6. What assurance does this Scripture give to believers on both sides of the issue?

7. How should that assurance affect our attitude toward a Christian we disagree with?

♦ **8.** Christians who differ with us probably also have Scriptures to back up what they believe and do. What does that tell us about scriptural clarity on certain issues?

♦ **9.** Put your own "favorite" disputable issue into this Scripture. What principles does this Scripture give you for dealing with Christians who see that issue differently?

♦ **10.** The chapter begins with "Accept . . . ." If acceptance is not to provide a forum for a debate, what *should* follow our acceptance of a Christian with whom we disagree?

11. Think back to the item you chose in question 1. If you have been thinking or behaving in an unaccepting manner toward another believer over this issue, what can you do to remedy it?

CAN WE JUDGE ANOTHER'S MOTIVES?

Romans 14:5-12

Someone observed it's a pity human beings can't exchange places, for everyone knows exactly how the *other* person should be. It seems to be an irresistible part of human nature to judge others' actions and motives. We like to think we're better than others, but the truth is that we all stand on equal ground before God.

The first Christians were Jews. The issue of how "Jewish" a Christian had to be was a recurring question in the early church. In a mixed Jewish-Gentile church such as in Rome, conflicts and judgments over Jewish holy days and dietary laws could be expected. The principles Paul gave for handling those conflicts also speak to us today.

1. What are some of the issues Christians in your church disagree about?

Read Romans 14:5-12.

2. In verse 5 Paul says, "Each one should be fully convinced in his own mind." Convinced of what?

3. What positive allowances does Paul make about the motives of the people on both sides of these arguments (verses 6-8)?

♦ **4.** What should be our motivation for *any* action?

5. Under what circumstances, if any, should we try to determine another's motivation for an action? Discuss situations in which you might be justified in inquiring about someone's beliefs or reasons for doing something.

6. In verses 5-7, Paul writes about accepting one another. We might expect him next to say something like, "So remember we all need each other." Instead, where does he turn the argument next? Why?

7. How can recognizing the truths of verses 8-9 help Christians accept each other?

♦ **8.** Verse 11 is a quote from Isaiah 45:23, a passage about God's judgment on the nations (unbelievers). Why might Paul pull that quote into a discussion of disagreement among believers?

9. How does knowing that we all must give our own account to God help us look at other Christians with whom we differ (verses 10-12)?

10. Has another Christian ever misunderstood your motives for doing something? How did you handle the situation?

11. Think of a time when you have misunderstood another person's motives or actions. How can Paul's exhortations help you deal with differences?

WHAT IF WE SEE A CHRISTIAN SINNING?

1 Corinthians 5; 2 Corinthians 2:5-11

In our society today tolerance has become a high virtue—tolerance of others' rights, religions, and lifestyles. The pressure to live and let live is great. Last week's study challenged us to respect one another's conscience and leave each other alone with our personal decisions about conduct.

But what do we do when people quote Scripture to justify racism, abortion, and homosexual marriages? How should we respond when we see a Christian doing something we think is sin—something beyond the gray areas of conscience?

1. Do you hesitate to confront a fellow believer who is doing something wrong? Why or why not?

Read 1 Corinthians 5.

2. With what overall tone does Paul address the Corinthians?

♦ **3.** What had the Corinthian Christians failed to do, which Paul thought necessary and urgent?

♦ **4.** Paul considered this particular sin bad enough to call for discipline within the church. What was Paul's objective in encouraging this strong discipline (verses 5-8)?

5. What is the only distinction made between the people in verse 10 and the person in verse 11? Why is this important?

♦ **6.** Paul does not sound very "accepting" in verse 11. What harm can result from overlooking sin among Christians?

♦ **7.** What sort of sins does your church confront with church discipline? Why is church discipline a rarity today?

8. How do you decide which sins are "big league" enough to alter your fellowship with other Christians?

9. Think back to Romans 14. What are some differences between the situations described there and the situation in 1 Corinthians 5?

Read 2 Corinthians 2:5-11.

10. This passage appears to be a follow-up of the discipline situation in 1 Corinthians 5. How are love and acceptance to be in evidence even in cases of discipline?

♦ **11.** If you had to approach the person discussed in this chapter, what would you do and say?

CAN'T I DO WHAT I WANT TO DO?

Romans 14:13-18

Awareness of individual and civil rights has become a permanent part of the fabric of our culture. Certainly it is important to promote fairness and equality. But often the "rights" rhetoric becomes a cover for selfishness, power, and sin.

This is where the rules of the kingdom of heaven clash with our cultural values. Jesus calls us to die to ourselves, so we shouldn't be surprised when that includes being more concerned for another's well-being than our own. Sometimes we must let go of our rights out of love and concern for others.

1. Shouldn't I be able to do what God says is all right for me to do? Discuss.

Read Romans 14:13-18.

2. Verse 13 is addressed to both the DO-ers and the DON'T-ers—those who feel free to do what they think is right, and those who tend to be judgmental. What is Paul's advice to each? What is involved in "making up your mind"?

3. How is it possible to injure another believer by what you do, even though your own conscience is clear?

4. What is the relationship between my action and my brother or sister's convictions (verses 14-16)?

5. Verses 15-16 use some strong language. Do you think Paul was overstating his case for emphasis? Give some reasons for your answer.

♦ **6.** How could one Christian's personal freedom destroy another believer? How could it damage the gospel in others' eyes (verse 16)?

♦ **7.** What's the difference between offending an overly touchy believer and actually doing damage to someone else's conscience?

♦ **8.** Why is acting in love of greater importance than our doing our own thing?

9. Relate a time, without using names, when another believer's free action set you back in your own walk with the Lord, or when you have hurt another Christian by doing something you felt guiltless about. How did you handle the situation?

10. What perspective does Paul offer in verses 17-18? How can we please God in these matters?

WHAT DOES STUMBLING MEAN?

Romans 14:19-23

"I am a rock. I am an island." So goes a well-known folk song. But we don't live our Christian lives as isolated "islands." We are all together in the same boat. We need each other and what one of us does affects all of us for good or for bad.

Such a community awareness goes against the individualism of our age. We would prefer to assert ourselves and say, "I can do what I want." Paul says that kind of thinking taken to the extreme can wreak havoc in the church. We must often do what we *don't* want to do, for the sake of our brothers and sisters in Christ.

1. Give an example of a good object used in a wrong or harmful way.

36

Read Romans 14:19-23.

2. Paul urges his readers to make every possible effort toward peace and mutual edification. What are some examples of actions that lead to these desirable results?

3. Think of an issue that divides the Christians in your community. Rewrite verse 20, substituting this issue for "food." What light does this shed on the dispute?

♦ **4.** Look back at your answer to question 1. How does it fit with Paul's statement "All food is clean, but it is wrong for a man to eat anything that causes someone else to stumble"?

5. Christians often argue about what is right to *do* and what actions are allowable. Paul says it's right *not* to do something. What is it?

6. What might causing someone to "stumble" or "fall" mean in this context?

◆ **7.** What particular message is here for Christians who like to flaunt their freedom verbally? How would this help keep the peace?

◆ **8.** What is the important deciding factor for our actions in disputable matters (verse 23)?

◆ **9.** If we encourage a person to participate in something he's not sure is right, how do we endanger him? How do we endanger ourselves?

10. We are challenged to pursue things that make for *mutual* edification. If we live by the principles of this passage, how will weaker Christians be encouraged and built up by us? How will we be built up by them?

11. As we aim for Christian unity, we often feel that we'd have oneness if only other Christians would adopt *our* firm convictions, or would loosen up and enjoy *our* freedoms. How does this entire chapter refute that idea? What is Paul's alternative method of achieving oneness?

FOLLOWING JESUS' EXAMPLE

Romans 15:1-7

The person who lives only for himself is engaged in a very small business. The business of the kingdom is larger and grander than our puny selves. And against our self-centered individualism stands the example of Christ, who lived for others. We cannot claim to follow him while deliberately doing things that injure others. By following his example of selfless living, we'll be led toward greater unity.

1. How can power be used to hurt others, even in the spiritual arena?

Read Romans 15:1-7.

2. Why do the "strong" have a particular temptation to please themselves instead of pleasing their neighbors?

3. In what ways is it *dis*pleasing to ourselves to put up with other Christians' failings?

◆ **4.** From what you know about the life of Christ, give some examples of how he put up with people's failings or weaknesses and still accepted them.

5. If you wish, give an example of how you have experienced Christ's acceptance, even with *your* failings (the more recent, the better).

6. What is the source of our hope?

7. Why do we need "endurance" and "encouragement" to live in unity with each other in Christ (verses 4-5)?

8. Why isn't unity automatic as soon as people become Christians?

9. Paul tells us to glorify the Lord "with one heart and mouth" (verse 6). When we glorify the Lord with one *mouth* (verbally) but not with one *heart* (inwardly), what are the results?

10. Why are we to accept others (verse 7)? What are some difficulties you have in accepting other believers? Be specific.

11. How does Christ's acceptance of you encourage you to respond to those Christians you find particularly difficult to accept?

BUT DON'T I KNOW BEST?

1 Corinthians 8:1-8

Corinth was a commercial and cultural center in ancient Greece. Its population was mixed—Roman, Greek, and Oriental, and it was infamous for its immorality and pagan worship. The Corinthian church included former pagans and idol-worshipers among its membership, as well as free thinkers, intellectuals, and people of varied cultural backgrounds. In other words, Corinth was a place ripe for religious conflicts—and therefore an ideal place to learn and to demonstrate unity and tolerance for one another's Christian conscience.

In Corinth, meat was offered in pagan sacrifices, and then the meat was sold at bargain prices. This presented a problem: should Christians purchase such "idol-tainted" meat and make dinner out of it?

1. Name some convictions other Christians hold which you consider overly strict.

Read 1 Corinthians 8:1-8.

◆ **2.** Paul was familiar with the more liberal Corinthians' argument *for* the freedom to eat meat that had been sacrificed to idols. He quoted it back to them in verses 4-6. What was their argument for liberality?

3. What did Paul find to agree with in their stand?

4. How did he poke some holes in their argument?

♦ **5.** What are some dangers and temptations which go along with possessing knowledge and insight?

6. In their arguments for freedom, the Corinthians had overlooked one consideration. How did Paul bring it up?

♦ **7.** Wouldn't it help the former idol-worshipers to be shown that they had unnecessary fears, and to be encouraged to eat this meat?

8. In verse 8, how does Paul draw the focus away from the meat itself and onto the Corinthian brothers and sisters in Christ?

9. What are some present-day issues in which Christians overemphasize the details of the issue and overlook the feelings and needs of other believers?

10. Some think that the mark of a mature Christian is freedom from restrictive hang-ups and legalism. Instead of an attitude of superiority, what attitude does Paul instruct the Corinthians to cultivate?

11. In what area of your Christian experience do you lack acceptance or compassion for more restrictive Christians? How can you demonstrate love in that specific situation?

WHEN DO I GIVE IN?

1 Corinthians 8:9-13

Because of our varied backgrounds we all have certain assumptions and convictions that determine our choices. When someone's convictions differ from ours, we are often quick to question the genuineness of his or her faith. And some people's faith has been sent reeling by another's questionable behavior.

Paul continues his argument for self-restriction for the sake of those with more tender consciences. The dangers are very real. His strong language might make us uncomfortable, but we need to hear his appeal and take it seriously.

1. Give a working definition of *Christian freedom.*

Read 1 Corinthians 8:9-13.

2. Review 1 Corinthians 8:1-8. What is the "freedom" Paul's readers enjoyed?

♦ 3. How would you define a "weak conscience"?

♦ 4. We can imagine the Corinthians objecting along these lines: "If my brother has a weak conscience, I'll help him strengthen it by breaking him in so he learns he can do the things he imagines are wrong." How would Paul have countered such an objection?

5. Pick out Paul's strong warnings in verses 11-12. What basic Christian values are at the heart of these warnings?

♦ **6.** If every freedom has a corresponding responsibility, what was the responsibility Paul laid at the door of the Corinthians who weren't bothered by eating meat sacrificed to idols?

7. In verse 13, Paul vowed lifelong abstinence from meat if he had to choose between eating meat and making his Christian brother stumble. Do you think he *really* meant: "I will never eat meat *while my weaker brother is looking"*? Why?

8. Make a case for abstaining from a freedom only when you might be observed by a weaker Christian. Make a case for abstaining all the time, even when you won't be observed by a weaker Christian.

9. Discuss the following case study.

You are a Christian who feels free to enjoy an occasional glass of wine with a meal. You have never been drunk, overindulgence does not tempt you, and you never drink alone. You are in a restaurant about to order wine with your meal, when another believer whom you know takes a nearby table and greets you. You know that this person is a recovering alcoholic. What do you do?

___ Order nothing alcoholic, because if you do, your friend will be tempted.

___ Go ahead, because your friend needs to get used to seeing other people drink; otherwise he shouldn't be coming to restaurants where alcohol is served at all.

___ It depends on the stage of the other person's recovery and how susceptible he is to the temptation to drink.

____ Regardless of the stage of my friend's recovery, I should abstain to show my support of him.

____ It depends on whether he already knows that I drink. If it would shock him to see me, I should not order the wine.

____ Alternative answers:

10. Come up with your own case study, perhaps based on an actual experience, that would require using these principles of Christian freedom.

WHY DO EYES NEED EARS?

1 Corinthians 12:12-26

A person missing some part of his body is considered handicapped or disabled. The person can—and must—learn to cope and manage life as well as possible; other parts of the body take over, or he uses special aids. Still that part of his body is clearly lacking.

The church is like a human body, with Christ as its head. We all have a part to play to benefit the whole body. If we fail to see ourselves as part of the unified whole, fitting in and doing our job, then the whole body suffers.

1. Have you ever been on a committee in which one person didn't do his or her job? What were the results?

Read 1 Corinthians 12:12-26.

◆ **2.** Verse 13 mentions four groups of people. What is significant about these groups being united in Christ? Who binds us together into one body?

◆ **3.** What kinds of people who naturally would have nothing in common does Christ bring together today? List some Christian friends with whom you would not be close (maybe would not even have met) if it were not for Christ.

4. In a word or phrase, describe the mistaken attitude of the "foot" and the "ear" in verses 15-16.

5. Have you ever found yourself feeling "out of it" in the church because you couldn't do a certain job? Share briefly about your experience and feelings.

◆ **6.** What reassurance does this passage give to Christians who feel useless to the Lord because they don't have certain "glamorous" talents?

7. What mistaken attitude do the "eye" and the "head" express in verse 21?

8. How might God give "greater honor to the parts that lacked it" in the body of Christ (verse 24)?

◆ **9.** What is God's purpose in combining many different parts together in the church (verses 25-26)?

◆ **10.** What sort of people do you consider unimportant in God's kingdom? Why? What attitude does your church communicate about differing gifts and abilities?

11. If you have experienced suffering in which other members of Christ's body suffered with you (verse 26), tell about it.

Tell about a time when you have been honored and other members of the body rejoiced with you.

12. Perhaps you know a believer who is hurting. How can you share in that believer's suffering and fulfill verse 26?

13. How can you honor another believer?

WHAT HAPPENS IF I DON'T FORGIVE?

Ephesians 4:25-32

By this point in your study, you may be thinking, "All this theory about Christian unity is great, but I don't see it happening. I see quarreling and bitterness among Christians just like the rest of the world."

The reality is that we experience Christian *dis*unity as much as we experience Christian unity. If Christian unity were easy and natural, Christ wouldn't have needed to pray for it, Paul wouldn't have needed to write about, and you wouldn't have to be studying it. Getting along in any relationship takes working at love and forgiveness.

1. How have your attitudes toward disunity among Christians changed in these past weeks?

Read Ephesians 4:25-32.

♦ **2.** Identify the three problem areas Paul discusses in
verses 25-28. How do these sins split up the body of
Christ?

♦ **3.** Using verse 29 as your model, brainstorm some practical guidelines for talk and conversation among Christians.
(Example: "Is what I'm about to say completely true?")

♦ **4.** Why would disunity among Christians particularly
grieve the Spirit of God?

5. How do the disasters of verse 31 arise among Christians?

6. When we've been hurt by other Christians, we're to forgive "just as in Christ God forgave [us]" (verse 32). What often keeps you from forgiving others?

7. Think of some phrases, either from Scripture or in your own words, that describe God's forgiveness in Christ. If we apply these phrases to situations of offense between Christians, how will our unity be nurtured?

8. If you are facing a situation in which you have suffered hurt at the hands of another believer, what practical help does this passage offer you?

9. What are some particular steps you can take toward restoring unity in this situation?

10. Review what we are to "put off" and "get rid of." Which of these areas are you struggling the most with right now? Pray together, asking God to help you act lovingly in relationships.

IS TENSION HEALTHY?

Galatians 5:13-26

These past weeks you've considered ways to "keep the unity of the Spirit through the bond of peace" (Ephesians 4:3). You've seen that it's possible to be true to your own conscience while making allowances for other people's viewpoints. You've pondered the heart-attitude that brings about unity in the midst of diversity.

Now go on to seek deeper unity with others in Christ. You can expect spiritual opposition—from Satan and from your own sinful nature. We tend to go to extremes, and the quest for unity has its dangers on both ends. But the tension can be healthy, since it keeps us from taking our task of unity too lightly.

1. What barriers to "keeping the unity of the Spirit" do you still see in yourself? In your church? Among the Christians in your community?

Read Galatians 5:13-26.

◆ **2.** In Romans 14 and 1 Corinthians 8 you saw that freedom of conscience should be curbed when it might damage another believer. How does Galatians 5:13-15
confirm and add to that principle?

◆ **3.** Even when we want to practice love and acceptance toward other believers, what forces stand in our way (verses
16-17)?

4. Identify the sins that can damage Christian unity from
the list in verses 19-21. Why would these destroy oneness?

5. The good news is that the qualities listed as the fruit of the Spirit lead to Christian oneness. How would these attitudes affect the destructive acts listed previously?

6. What is the source of attitudes which will foster Christian unity?

♦ **7.** How do we crucify the sinful nature (verse 24)? Why is this an important aspect of unity?

8. When we think of being led by the Spirit, we often think of questions like "What should I do today?" and "Where should I go?" Taking this passage as a whole, and particularly verses 25-26, what does it mean to keep in step with the Spirit?

♦ **9.** Choose one of the current barriers to unity you identified in question 1. What action can you take to overcome this roadblock and foster the "unity of the Spirit through the bond of peace"?

10. Read Romans 15:5-6 together as a closing benediction.

LEADER'S NOTES

■ **Study 1/That All of Them May Be One**

Question 4. "Eternal life is best seen not as everlasting life but as knowledge of the Everlasting One. To know God transforms a person and introduces him to a life he could not otherwise experience. . . . The way in which men come to have eternal life is by coming to know God by coming to know Jesus" (D.A. Carson, *The Farewell Discourse and Final Prayer of Jesus,* pp. 180–81. Grand Rapids, Mich.: Baker Book House, 1980).

Question 6. We should not "suppose that because Jesus here prays exclusively for his disciples he therefore has no concern for the world. . . . The fact of the matter is that Jesus must have some concern for the world or he would not be found praying for his followers to bear appropriate witness to the world. . . . Jesus could not possibly be praying for the world in the same way that he is praying for his disciples. . . . The only thing that Jesus could be praying with respect to the world is precisely that the world cease to be the world" *(The Farewell Discourse and Final Prayer of Jesus,* p. 187).

■ Study 2/The Do-ers and the Don't-ers

Question 2. "Eating 'everything' may refer to freedom from dietary restrictions, or it may refer to eating meat offered to idols, while the person weaker in the faith eats only vegetables and refuses to eat meat that has been offered to idols. . . . After a sacrifice was presented to a god in a pagan temple, only part of it was burned. The remainder was often sent to the market to be sold. Thus a Christian might easily—unknowingly—buy such meat" *(Life Application Bible,* p. 2053. Wheaton, Ill.: Tyndale House Publishers, 1991).

Question 5. Weak in faith can imply "a lack of balance in discerning between the essentials and non-essentials of saving and sanctifying faith" *(The New Bible Commentary: Revised,* p. 1042. Grand Rapids, Mich.: Wm. B. Eerdmans Publishing Co., 1970).

Question 8. While it's possible to twist Scripture deliberately and take it out of context, Bible-believing Christians sincerely come to varying interpretations of Scripture. Some questions have no clear black-and-white answers in Scripture. Ironically, some issues that we think are the clearest are also the most disputed (for example, baptism, Communion, church government).

Question 9. Paul emphasized the willingness to look beyond the *issue* to the *person.*

Question 10. Though there are some issues that are foundational to our faith, many others are simply based on individual convictions. Our principle should be: in essentials, unity; in nonessentials, liberty; in everything, love.

■ Study 3/Can We Judge Another's Motives?

Question 4. Our motivation should be to honor the Lord and give thanks to God. Note that different people can be doing different things for the same motivation. "Paul becomes gripped with this normative principle of inspiration of service and expands it in these verses. The Lordship of Christ is supreme and all-inclusive of life and death and judgment" *(New Bible Commentary: Revised,* p. 1043).

Question 8. Read Isaiah 45:22-25 for the context. (Paul quoted from the Greek version of the Old Testament rather than the Hebrew, which may explain the inexact quote.) Perhaps his point is that even nonbelievers will eventually have to acknowledge God, so we shouldn't be too worried about believers; the Lord will show them if they're wrong.

■ Study 4/What If We See a Christian Sinning?

Question 3. Paul writes this to the church in the city of Corinth, a major trade center and a city filled with much idolatry and immorality. The church was made up of mostly converted Gentiles, and it looks like the church was overly influenced by its environment.

Question 4. "To 'hand this man over to Satan' means to exclude him from the fellowship of believers. Without the spiritual support of Christians, this man would be left alone with his sin and Satan, and perhaps this emptiness would drive him to repentance. . . . Putting someone out of the church should be a last resort, . . . done out of love . . . to correct and restore. The church's role should be to help, not hurt, offenders, motivating them to repent of their sins and return to the fellowship of the church" *(Life Application Bible,* p. 2068).

Question 6. See 1 Corinthians 5:6. If flagrant sin is not dealt with, it influences everything and everyone around it. The caution would apply to unrepentant sinners, not to those who have repented and are trying to overcome their sins. While accepting sinners, we must also be careful about their potential influence.

Question 7. Some members may draw a blank because they've never seen their churches discipline anyone—either because their members live uprightly or because they tolerate sin. Most churches have some transgression at least "on the books" which call for dismissing members (unless they repent).

Question 11. For further study, Matthew 18:15-35 is a helpful passage on confrontation, judgment, and forgiveness.

■ Study 5/Can't I Do What I Want To Do?

Question 6. "To allow one's *good,* i.e. one's liberty, to grieve and destroy others in this way would cause the gospel to be spoken of as evil" *(New Bible Commentary: Revised,* p. 1943).

Question 7. Some Christians are distressed about nearly *everything* others do, and constantly find fault. They seem to make a career out of being offended! Are you leading them into sin or simply offending their traditions? In either case the challenge is to act in love.

Question 8. The motive for deferring to the weaker brother's opinion is the overruling principle of love. Paul here connects this with the fact that this brother also shares in the benefits and atonement of Christ's death.

■ Study 6/What Does Stumbling Mean?

Question 4. Paul might have said, "That VCR by itself is fine, but it is wrong to lead anyone into sin by what you show on it." God-given things become bad when they're used wrongly.

Question 7. You know the type: "I was taught that I couldn't dance, I couldn't drink, I couldn't go to the theater"—so they do all three in excess to show off their newfound freedom and "maturity." Paul challenges them to lift their eyes from their own rights to the needs of others.

Question 8. "Faith, i.e. in this context conviction and fixed principle, is the all-important factor. To change one's behavior in such a matter without believing that it is the right thing to do is, in fact, sin" *(New Bible Commentary: Revised,* p. 1043).

Question 9. We can endanger another person by encouraging him to knowingly violate his conscience. He will either suffer from guilt or he will become casual about sin and perhaps go further into it. We open ourselves to the temptation of pride because we helped a less enlightened person "see the light." We damage our own relationship with God by sinning against a brother.

■ Study 7/Following Jesus' Example

Question 4. Even when people were slow to understand or lacked belief, Jesus did not withdraw his love (Luke 9:41). When Peter denied him, Jesus showed his love for him in a special way later (John 18; 21). The best example of his love may be the statement at his crucifixion, "Father, forgive them . . ." (Luke 23:34).

■ Study 8/But Don't I Know Best?

Question 2. They argued that they were enlightened, the idols were unreal, and God is Lord of all.

Question 5. "Love is more important than knowledge. Knowledge can make us look good and feel important, but we can all too easily develop an arrogant, know-it-all attitude. Many people with strong opinions are unwilling to listen to and learn from God and others" *(Life Application Bible,* p. 2074).

Question 7. First they needed to come to their own convictions, led by the Holy Spirit. Dragging them into halfhearted, guilty participation would not be helpful. You might refer again to Romans 14:23.

■ Study 9/When Do I Give In?

Question 3. From this Scripture passage a weak conscience would be one which sees sin where others see innocence.

Question 4. Though Paul stood against legalism, it's interesting that here he did not scold the overscrupulous for being legalistic. Instead he called for respect. He recognized actual spiritual harm that could come to the sensitive person who violates his conscience.

Question 6. "Christian freedom does not mean that anything goes. . . . It is inseparably tied to Christian responsibility. . . . Some actions may be perfectly all right for us to do, but may harm a Christian brother or sister who is still young in faith. . . . When we love others, our freedom should be less important to us than strengthening the faith of a brother or sister in Christ" *(Life Application Bible,* p. 2074).

■ Study 10/Why Do Eyes Need Ears?

Question 2. Different races, economic levels, ages, social strata, and life experiences are brought together in Christ. The Holy Spirit incorporates us into the body of Christ. "The Spirit is around us (the figure of immersion in water) and within us (the figure of drinking)" *(New Bible Commentary: Revised,* p. 1067).

Question 3. If your Christian friends are all the same age, background, and social status that you are, you may be experiencing "fellowship" on a human level rather than supernatural unity in Christ. Some church programs group people by social similarities and don't give Christian oneness much chance to operate.

Question 6. Each one is equally and fully part of Christ's body. The body needs more than those "glamorous" talents; everyone has a part.

Question 9. For further study on the interworking of various gifts in the body of Christ, study Ephesians 4:1-16.

Question 10. Ask secondary questions: Are there people who don't seem to have anything to contribute to the work of Christ? Are there people or social groups you overlook when Bible study groups are formed? In any church there are individuals or even whole families who "fall through the cracks" for years and never find a niche. If we live in Christian oneness, those people will be included.

■ Study 11/What Happens If I Don't Forgive?

Question 2. Lying shows disdain for the person lied to and destroys trust. Nursing anger exaggerates the original offense as you replay it in your mind. Dishonest practices "use" other people for gain and create distrust.

Question 3. We can't go down a lengthy checklist every time we open our mouths, but we can internalize some principles to guide our conversation.

Question 4. "Foul or inappropriate language is not only an insult to the hearer; it saddens the Holy Spirit by wounding Him and denying in practice the meaning of His indwelling and sanctifying presence in the believer, which is a token of his final redemption" *(New Bible Commentary: Revised,* p. 1118). See Ephesians 1:13-14.

■ Study 12/Is Tension Healthy?

Question 2. Our freedom must be tempered with love. We're free to do good, not to sin.

Question 3. Our own sin nature is still alive and well. So is Satan. So is everybody else's sin nature.

Question 7. When we become Christians we turn from our sins to Christ as Savior. But we still struggle with our sinful nature. "As Christians we still have the capacity to sin, but we have been set free from sin's power over us and no longer have to give in to it. We must daily commit our sinful tendencies to God's control, daily crucify them, and moment by moment draw on the Spirit's power to overcome them" *(Life Application Bible,* p. 2126).

Question 9. Action can be *internal*: changing negative thoughts about a particular person or group, praying for Christians in conflict, forgiving another believer, deciding to overlook doctrinal differences; or *external*: starting an inter-denominational prayer group, studying other Christian traditions, curbing negative talk about other churches, seeking out fellowship with Christians who don't see things exactly like you do, or working for cooperation among churches in your community for Christmas or Easter services, a choir festival, evangelistic meetings, a film series.

WHAT SHOULD WE STUDY NEXT?

To help your group answer that question, we've listed the Fisherman Guides by category so you can choose your next study.

TOPICAL STUDIES

Angels, Wright

Becoming Women of Purpose, Barton

Building Your House on the Lord, Brestin

The Creative Heart of God, Goring

Discipleship, Reapsome

Doing Justice, Showing Mercy, Wright

Encouraging Others, Johnson

The End Times, Rusten

Examining the Claims of Jesus, Brestin

Friendship, Brestin

The Fruit of the Spirit, Briscoe

Great Doctrines of the Bible, Board

Great Passages of the Bible, Plueddemann

Great Prayers of the Bible, Plueddemann

Growing Through Life's Challenges, Reapsome

Guidance & God's Will, Stark

Heart Renewal, Goring

Higher Ground, Brestin

Integrity, Engstrom & Larson

Lifestyle Priorities, White

Marriage, Stevens

Miracles, Castleman

One Body, One Spirit, Larson

The Parables of Jesus, Hunt

Prayer, Jones

The Prophets, Wright

Proverbs & Parables, Brestin

Satisfying Work, Stevens & Schoberg

Senior Saints, Reapsome

Sermon on the Mount, Hunt

A Spiritual Legacy, Christensen

Spiritual Warfare, Moreau

The Ten Commandments, Briscoe

Who Is God? Seemuth

Who Is Jesus? Van Reken

Who Is the Holy Spirit? Knuckles & Van Reken

Wisdom for Today's Woman: Insights from Esther, Smith

Witnesses to All the World, Plueddemann

Worship, Sibley

BIBLE BOOK STUDIES

Genesis, Fromer & Keyes
Exodus, Larsen
Job, Klug
Psalms, Klug
Proverbs: Wisdom That Works,
 Wright
Jeremiah, Reapsome
Jonah, Habakkuk, & Malachi,
 Fromer & Keyes
Matthew, Sibley
Mark, Christensen
Luke, Keyes
John: Living Word, Kuniholm
Acts 1-12, Christensen
Paul (Acts 13-28), Christiansen
Romans: The Christian
 Story, Reapsome
1 Corinthians, Hummel

Strengthened to Serve
 (2 Corinthians),
 Plueddemann
Galatians, Titus & Philemon,
 Kuniholm
Ephesians, Baylis
Philippians, Klug
Colossians, Shaw
Letters to the Thessalonians,
 Fromer & Keyes
Letters to Timothy, Fromer &
 Keyes
Hebrews, Hunt
James, Christensen
1 & 2 Peter, Jude, Brestin
How Should a Christian Live?
 (1, 2 & 3 John), Brestin
Revelation, Hunt

BIBLE CHARACTER STUDIES

David: Man after God's Own
 Heart, Castleman
Elijah, Castleman
Great People of the Bible,
 Plueddemann
King David: Trusting God for
 a Lifetime, Castleman
Men Like Us, Heidebrecht &
 Scheuermann

Moses, Asimakoupoulos
Paul (Acts 13-28), Christensen
Ruth & Daniel, Stokes
Women Like Us, Barton
Women Who Achieved for
 God, Christensen
Women Who Believed God,
 Christensen

Printed in the United States
by Baker & Taylor Publisher Services